STEAM'S LAMENT
British Railways Standard Pacifics

Kevin Derrick

Strathwood

STEAM'S LAMENT

British Railways Standard Pacifics

First published 2018
ISBN 1-905276-86-9
ISBN 978-1-905276-86-8

Published by Strathwood Publishing, 9 Boswell Crescent, Inverness, IV2 3ET
Telephone 01463 234004
Printed by Akcent Media, Ltd.

Contents **Page**

Celebrating all things Britannia

On show to the public within Doncaster Works on 27 September 1953, and 70000 Britannia is far from her pristine as new condition after thirty-two months in service based out of 30A Stratford. She was first seen out on the mainline leaving Crewe on a test run in unlined black on 12 January 1951. Her naming took place at Marylebone on 30 January 1951, resplendent in the then new lined green livery as the first brand new design since Nationalisation on 1 January 1948. In our second view 70000 Britannia doubles up with classmate 70050 Firth of Clyde as they conduct a shunting move within Willesden's shed yard in May 1964.
Rail Photoprints & Bob Treacher/Alton Model Centre

The second locomotive to enter service in February 1951, 70001 bore the name Lord Hurcomb, who was the British Transport Commission's chairman. This came about as part of the committee formed to allocate names to this new class of Pacifics which was formed in 1948, planned at one point to name 70000 as Lord Hurcomb, this was dropped firstly in favour of the name Great Britain to coincide with the Festival of Britain at the time. Then Riddles stepped in and pushed for the name Britannia to be adopted instead, taking the name away from the Jubilee 45700 with the same name, with the name of Amethyst being awarded to the 4-6-0 instead. Here we see 70001 Lord Hurcomb firstly on shed at 32A Norwich in March 1960 and then light engine at Bletchley in 1963.
Both: Strathwood Library Collection

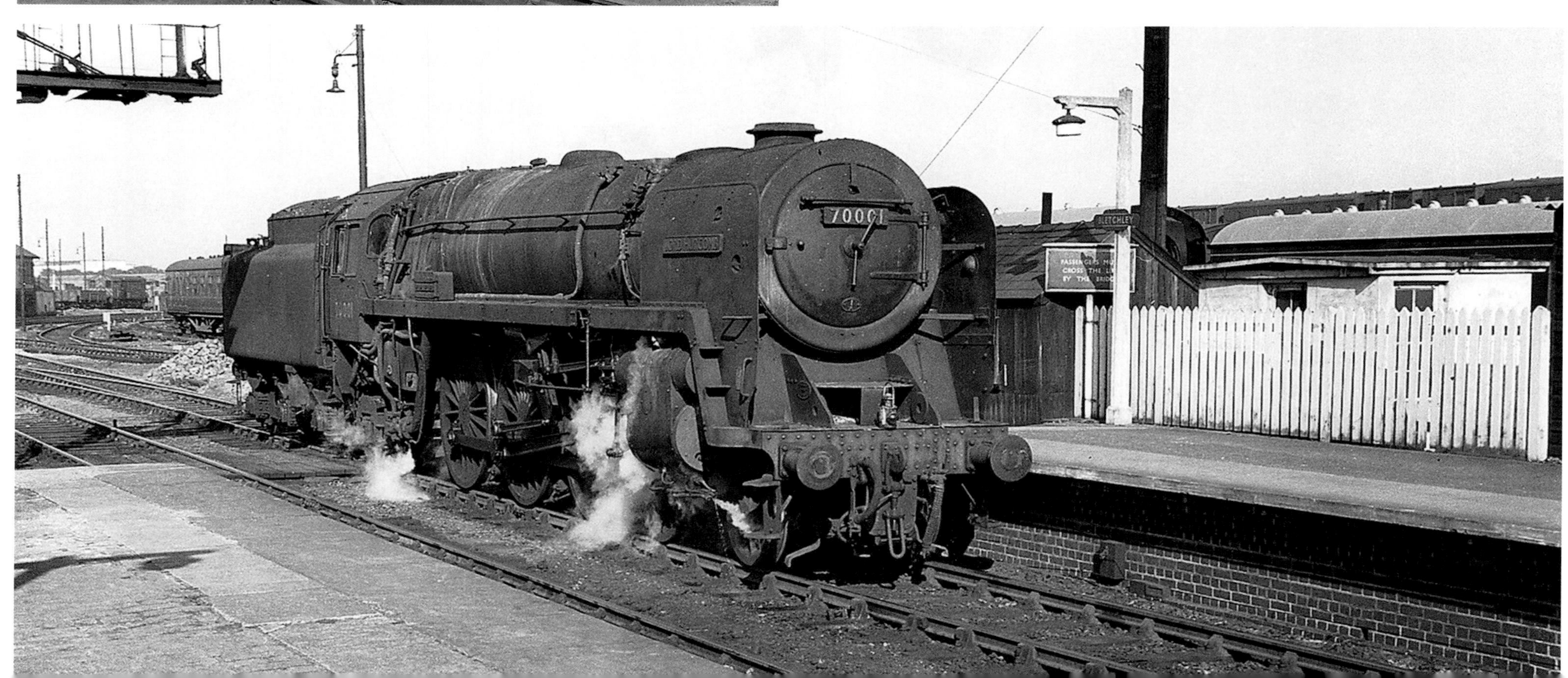

In March 1951 70002 went into service from Crewe Works with the name Geoffrey Chaucer as the first of a good number of poets and playwrights to be so honoured. In 1959, 70002 was still Eastern Region allocated when recorded at 31B March. The first fourteen deliveries of the Britannias went to 30A Stratford and 32A Norwich Thorpe to help speed up express services between London and East Anglia. In turn deliveries of Type 3 and Type 4 diesel locomotives from English Electric would soon make them surplus to this area. ***Strathwood Library Collection***

Standards of cleanliness have certainly slipped for 70002 Geoffrey Chaucer by the time of this next view taken in 1964 on shed at 2J Aston. What would become the locomotives last reallocation to 12A Carlisle Kingmoor had already taken place in December the year previously, with 70002 being withdrawn in January 1967. ***Rail Online***

Opposite: Next to appear on stage would be 70003 John Bunyan, entering traffic as the second of three Britannias released from Crewe in March 1951. On 31 March 1962, 70003 was to be found on rail tour duty at Thetford with a tour organised by the RCTS to commemorate the end of steam haulage on the Great Eastern Mainline, already a nail into the Britannia's coffins. ***Colour Rail***

THETFORD
RCTS
70003
JOHN BUNYAN
70003

Passengers are being told to keep their heads back as this service train slowly passes the derailed 70003 John Bunyan at Hellifield on 7 April 1966, after the Britannia's brakes had failed whilst working a freight she was put down a loop to allow Mother Nature to bring her to a halt safely. She was soon back at work and not withdrawn for another eleven months. *Peter Coton*

Opposite: Originally to have been part of the first batch of Britannias to go to the Eastern Region, 70004 William Shakespeare was nominally allocated to 30A Stratford, however, after she was given a special exhibition level of paintwork and metal burnishing, 70004 went directly to the Festival of Britain exhibition at Marylebone Station, arriving there on the 2 April 1951. In September 1951, 70004 took up service out of 73A Stewarts Lane becoming a regular on the Golden Arrow and is seen storming through Folkestone Warren in 1953 on just such a prestige duty. *Rail Photoprints*

GOLDEN
ARROW

In our first view of 70004, she had the Southern Region's longer front lamp brackets, and a shorter vacuum hose fixing, now in this view at Dover Marine from the same year we can see the long vacuum hose connection, shorter lamp brackets among the many small modifications made during these early years. The most notable being the examinations to find the reason for 70004 to bend her coupling rods at speed whilst passing Headcorn with the Golden Arrow in her first weeks in service, resulting in all of the Britannias being temporarily withdrawn for upgrades. ***Rail Photoprints***

The days of burnished steel and glory days on the Southern Region may well have passed, but on 29 August 1959, 70004 William Shakespeare made an appearance as an exhibit once again, this time for the Derby Works Open Day. The original early style of tender emblem would remain until late 1963, whilst the original design of smoke deflector handrails being put to good use here would remain until the end in December 1967 when she was among the forty Britannias withdrawn that year. ***Rail Online***

Although 70005 John Milton was first allocated to 30A Stratford, it went for steaming capability testing at Rugby Testing Station during April and May 1951, then again in December 1951, leaving everyone content with the performance the Britannia boiler, which was said to be capable of any task that was asked of it. Certainly experienced gained from these extensive trials went towards the designing of the Class 9Fs. Coming towards the end of their brief heyday on the crack Great Eastern expresses and regular cleaning, 70005 is being turned on the vacuum turntable at Liverpool Street in 1959 in preparation for a return towards its home shed of 32A Norwich Thorpe. ***Rail Online***

Opposite: The early Britannias including 70006 Robert Burns were originally fitted with the troublesome low dome, but these were being changed as soon as possible from April 1951. Eight years later and 70006 was the penultimate Britannia to have the smoke deflectors modified, more on this to follow. The same visit in late 1959 to Doncaster Works also resulted in the AWS equipment being fitted along with a speedometer unit among its modifications. In 1965, 70006 Robert Burns shares a breather with a Black Five in the confines of Carlisle Citadel station. This would be the last year that many of the class would be seen wearing their nameplates as they were removed for safekeeping. On 20 May 1967, the locomotive was withdrawn from service and stored at Carlisle Kingmoor until October 1967 and then sold to J.McWilliams of Shettleston, in Glasgow, being just one of a large number of the class to be scrapped here.
Strathwood Library Collection

70006
1M21

The initial Britannia build program was authorised on 17 November 1949, for Crewe Works who completed 70007 Coeur-de-Lion on 25 April 1951 to Order No.E479/220 at a cost of £20,025. Part of the East Anglian fleet until December 1963, we see her first at Norwich in 1953, then as part of the Carlisle Kingmoor allocation at Falkland Junction shortly before being withdrawn on 19 June 1965. The shed Foreman at 32A Norwich Thorpe stated that this example was prone to cracks in its mainframe, which even with a number of works visits to try and rectify the problems ultimately led to it being the first of the class to be withdrawn, becoming the only Britannia to be taken out of service from Crewe Works, the locomotive was stored at Crewe South depot for a short time and brought back into the Works in July 1965 for cutting up. ***Photos: Rail Online & Colour Rail***

70007
76097

The single chimney was sufficient for the well respected Britannia design of boiler, in this view the splattering of limescale around the locomotive's whistle is apparent. The name for 70008 Black Prince was derived after Edward Woodstock, the eldest son of King Edward III and Philippa of Hainault, most appropriate for the engine whilst working to and from East Anglia. ***Rail Online***

Displaying an express headcode via two white discs 70008 Black Prince thunders through Bethnal Green on 22 March 1960, just as the new deliveries of diesel locomotives were beginning to encroach on Britannia duties out of Liverpool Street. ***Colour Rail***

The Southern's Class E4 is shunting the brand new 70009 Alfred the Great into position on 1 June 1951, for a display of modern traction being held at Eastbourne. Although 70009 was well received on the Southern Region and used extensively on The Bournemouth Belle, another well-chosen naming as King Alfred the Great was indeed the King of Wessex into which the Pullman service served. During this first six months of service in what was left of 1951, 70009 visited Crewe Works six times, and Stratford on three occasions plus repairs were carried out by Doncaster Works a further six times. As a result, the recorded mileages for 70009 were low for 1951 being 22,700, but much improved for 1953 at 77,500 and 63,300 miles for 1954 and then 67,000 for 1955. ***The Bluebell Museum Archive***

In the mid-summer of 1951, 70009 Alfred the Great gets the chance to excel on today's down Bournemouth Belle as departure time approaches. This locomotive was assigned to the Southern Region along with two other classmates; 70004 William Shakespeare and 70014 Iron Duke, but as this left a shortage of engines three Southern Region engines were loaned to Stratford; 34039 Boscastle, 34057 Biggin Hill and 34066 Spitfire to fill the breach.
Dave Cobbe Collection-Rail Photoprints

Opposite: An elevated view of a rather work weary 70010 Owen Glendower at Patricroft during 1965, serves to illustrate the economy unlined green livery repaints now being carried out during overhauls on the class at Crewe Works. But also following complaints from engine crews of draughty conditions in the cab creating a coal dust storm on the footplate, flexible cab sheets were fitted to BR1 tenders from 1953. Owen Glendower was the Welsh Chief (1350-1414) who conducted war against the English on the border between England and Wales.
Late Jim Carter/Rail Photoprints

70010

OXENHOLME No2
70011

Pausing a while at Cleethorpes whilst working the RCTS arranged North Lincolnshire Rail Tour on 2 October 1965 was 70012 John of Gaunt. The nameplates were nowhere to be seen when it appeared on show for the Derby Works Open Day the same year, however.
Both: Strathwood Library Collection

Opposite: Carlisle Kingmoor's Britannia 70011 Hotspur rounds the curve at Oxenholme in charge of an up Class H freight mid-morning on Saturday 7 March 1964, aptly demonstrating its mixed traffic capabilities. The locomotive was named after the late-medieval English nobleman Sir Henry Percy, otherwise known as Harry Hotspur or simply Hotspur. Nothing to do with the Class B17/6, 61670 which briefly carried the name of the North London football club!
Gordon Edgar Collection/Rail Photoprints

On 5 August 1967, 70012 John of Gaunt departs from Lancaster with the 10:35 Euston to Barrow express passenger working. On 19 September 1966, the same locomotive was seen dumped at Carlisle Kingmoor with a badly damaged cab, there is no sign of this damage at all in this view, so perhaps it was quickly repaired by using the spare cab from the earlier withdrawn and scrapped at Crewe Works, 70007 as the intact cab was noted lying about for some while after the remainder of the locomotive had been scrapped. John of Gaunt, 70012 remained in service to the last official day, 30 December 1967, thus enjoying the distinction of being the longest serving member of the class, after 70013 Oliver Cromwell. After being withdrawn 70012 was put into storage at Carlisle Kingmoor until the end of March 1968, when the locomotive was moved to T.W. Ward's of Beighton, in Sheffield for cutting up in April 1968.
Bill Wright

Opposite: A visit to Doncaster Works the previous month before this photograph of 70013 Oliver Cromwell was taken at 30A Stratford on 7 June 1959, had seen the fitting of AWS equipment along with the smoke deflectors being modified to the LMR 1 type. In all, twelve Britannias were so treated during 1959, ten of them at Doncaster; the remaining two 70024 and 70029 being modified by Swindon Works. Another visit to Doncaster would see a speedometer unit fitted in December 1960, while it is interesting to note that the locomotive's tender was recorded as changed four times during 1960 too!
Late Norman Browne

70013
70013

7
70013

Opposite: Although all of the Britannias were built at Crewe Works between 1951 and 1954, the bulk of the early heavy overhauls were carried out at either Swindon or Doncaster. Once all of the class had been centred upon the London Midland Region by 1963, the responsibility for major repairs was within Crewe Works. Overhauls to the Britannias after 1965 meant a return to traffic in unlined green livery. However, there was to be an exception as it was decided by the British Transport Commission to save one of the class for the National Collection. Originally 70000 Britannia was the obvious choice, being the very first British Railways Standard locomotive. However, due to its condition being unfavourable, 70013 Oliver Cromwell was selected for a final heavy overhaul and a return to service in lined green livery, in order to work the expected series of steam specials that were being considered for what was expected to be the final twelve months of steam operation. During this last twelve months 70013 Oliver Cromwell was generally well kept in readiness for rail tour duties, sometimes with its nameplates fitted and others without, just showing the painted name instead. Here one evening in 1968, the noted steam cameraman and footplate man Jim Carter took his opportunity to set up this fine shot on shed at Patricroft, having used a flash to illuminate the footplate for us.
Late Jim Carter/Rail Photoprints

The British Rail Scottish Region organised Grand Rail Tour No.5 is seen awaiting the start signal from platform 16 at Manchester Victoria station behind 70013 Oliver Cromwell, as witnessed by Jim Carter on 1 June 1968. The train would be banked by Newton Heath's Black 5, 44884 for the sharp climb away and up Miles Platting Bank, as the special worked its way eastwards towards Guide Bridge and beyond. Of particular note on 70013 is the damage to the offside front valance which has caused the headlamp to be sitting at a rather odd angle. Soon it would all be over and 70013 would become a legend as part of the final steam working as the Fifteen Guinea Special along with Black 5s, 44781, 44871 & 45110 on 11 August 1968. ***Late Jim Carter/Rail Online***

On 28 April 1968, the superbly turned out 70013 Oliver Cromwell worked the G C Enterprises North West Circular Tour throughout. Eagle-eyed readers will have spotted that by now the smoke box number plate is subtly different from the original we saw on page 25, it appears a new one was cast after the original disappeared in 1966. ***Tony Butcher***

Opposite: Stewarts Lane allocated Britannia Pacific 70014 Iron Duke makes an impressive sight as it runs through Folkestone Warren with the up Golden Arrow, during 1953. Along with 70004 William Shakespeare this pair were entrusted with this prestige Pullman working for almost seven years, albeit 70014 in the role of backup engine. ***Rail Photoprints***

GOLDEN
ARROW

Another use for 70014 Iron Duke whilst it was on the books at 73A Stewarts Lane was on Boat Train extras such as this one passing through Sandling heading for Victoria in 1953. A move to 9E Trafford Park ensued in June 1958 where we see her within the confines of Manchester London Road (now Piccadilly) in 1958, somewhat grubbier but retaining the fixings on its smoke deflectors for the Golden Arrows and around the smoke box dart for the famous headboard. ***Both: Rail Photoprints***

70014
10

A nice scene at Laira as Old Oak Common's 70015 Apollo has come off the coaling line and is now being prepared for its return back home to the Capital from Plymouth in the mid 1950s. Between its introduction in June 1951 to 1B Camden, 70015 would also do a spell at 30A Stratford before heading to the Western Region in August 1953. ***Rail Online***

Opposite: Now wearing the Western Region's preferred style of hand holds to its smoke deflectors 70015 Apollo waits at Sheffield before heading to Manchester with ecs, in 1960, notice also the modified style of top lamp bracket on the smoke box, now she is allocated to 9E Trafford Park. ***Rail Photoprints***

70015
70015

It seems that Britannias were a little lighter-weight around their front buffer beams than other types as many of the shots within this volume show examples of buckling due to no doubt to rough buffering up within engine sheds after dark, in July 1961, 70015 Apollo demonstrates her rough treatment as she passes Patricroft. ***Late Jim Carter/Rail Photoprints***

Opposite: Compare the brand new 70016 Ariel seen on shed at 67A Corkerhill in July 1951, she was sent on trial to the London Midland Region first of all, working from 20A Leeds Holbeck. This view also shows us the original fluted style of coupling rods which were changed to the stronger solid variety to cure just one of the Britannias many teething problems. ***Rail Online***

70016
ARIEL
70016

After a move from Leeds Holbeck to 30A Stratford in March 1952, the next move for 70016 Ariel would be to 83D Plymouth Laira in September 1953, later to be joined there by three other sister engines, the Britannias would find themselves displaced from top link workings from Plymouth down to Penzance and further away to Bristol and Paddington by the invading diesel-hydraulics in the late fifties. Also after visibility problems with the handrails on the smoke deflectors sited as part of the cause for the tragic Milton derailment near Didcot in 1955, Western Region men from Laira and Old Oak took a dislike to the Britannias. As their work diminished such displaced members of the class were sent to join those already at Cardiff Canton where the enginemen had soon recognised their initial allocation of five of the class as being useful additions to the existing Castles allocated there for use on the principal express workings. In this handsome photograph, 70016 now carries its 86C Canton shedplate and is in the fine condition that the engines from that shed were maintained as she runs through Patchway with the Red Dragon on 14 September 1959. ***Rail Online***

Opposite: All signs of that Western Region prestige and cleanliness have now been lost since transfer to the London Midland Region and 6G Llandudno Junction, as today's crew for 70016 Ariel at Patricroft in February 1963 look out for their colleague Jim Carter with his trusty camera.
Late Jim Carter/Rail Photoprints

70016

70017
ARROW
70017

Opposite: Conversely, after a recent works visit 70017 Arrow looks smart alongside the coaler at 5A Crewe North on 23 June 1962. Alas, as four years later and 70017's premature end transpired in August 1966, this followed an accident when the locomotive was hauling an empty coaching stock train from Glasgow to Morecambe and was involved in a heavy collision with a freight train at St. Michaels in Carlisle. The resulting damage to the front end was considered too costly to repair at that time, however, had this occurred two years prior then most certainly the repairs would have been approved. After recovery from the crash site, 70017 was seen at Carlisle Upperby in August 1966, and announced as withdrawn shortly after. Disposal was to J. Cashmore of Newport in February 1967. *Colour Rail*

Above: With the Western Region's favoured train reporting numbers in place, 70018 Flying Dutchman heads West from Reading around 1958. *Strathwood Library Collection*

Swindon Works requested Crewe Works to fit Western Region lamp irons and their preferred Automatic Train Control equipment with in-frame pipework to 70018 during construction, this raised the cost slightly to £20,144. Ironically this was removed when the engine left for the LMR to be later replaced with AWS equipment at Crewe. Where we see her soon after in 1963.
Late Alan H. Bryant ARP-Rail Photoprints

Perhaps it was a cop for the spotters on the platforms at Salisbury as they gaze upon 70019 Lightning from 86C Cardiff Canton on 13 June 1959. In our second view taken on 10 September the following year, 70019 has drawn a few more admirers now that she is somewhat cleaner having just arrived at Paddington with today's Red Dragon named service from Swansea arriving in the Capital in time for a late lunch. ***Both: Colour Rail***

THE RED DRAGON
A35
LIGHTNING
70019
4

REWE
CNJ58

Opposite: One of a batch of fifteen Britannias named after earlier famous GWR broad gauge locomotives, 70019 Lightning went new to 83A Newton Abbot in June 1951 before a transfer to 83D Plymouth Laira. On 28 August 1951, it became the first of the class to work the Cornish Riviera Express into Cornwall. All the Western Region Britannias went to Cardiff Canton in 1956 to concentrate them upon just one shed for maintenance. We see her now on the London Midland Region as there is time for some conversation in 1963 on the platforms at Crewe, as 70019 waits to head north.
Late Alan H. Bryant ARPS/Rail Photoprints

The requested motive power was 70020 Mercury seen running into Salisbury with the Southern Counties Touring Society's, The South Western Rambler Rail Tour on 8 March 1964. Waiting to take over the next leg was Class 9F 92209, after refuelling and servicing 70020 Mercury would meet the tour once again at Bournemouth Central for the run back to Waterloo.
Late Hugh Ballantyne/Rail Photoprints

Back on home territory once more on 9 May 1964, 70020 Lightning has just been cleaned once again. ***Colour Rail***

Opposite: Plymouth Laira based 70021 Morning Star puts on a good show passing through Hayle with the up Cornish Riviera Express on 30 July 1953. ***Rail Photoprints***

CORNISH RIVIERA
70021

Climbing well past Camden Goods Depot the driver of 70021 Morning Star seems happy with his progress as they leave London Euston with a Manchester-bound service on 21 July 1962. Perhaps its the fact that the engine was only shopped at Swindon Works twice and thereafter always at Crewe, is the reason that 70021 became the only Western Region Britannia to avoid the modification to the smoke deflectors.
Dave Cobbe/Rail Photoprints

In stark contrast to the earlier condition of Cardiff Canton's Britannias, 70022 Tornado storms east of Badminton with a Paddington to Fishguard relief service on 13 June 1959. She would become one of four Britannias to be perhaps unusually shedded at 2A Rugby in 1962, the others being 70017 Arrow, 70023 Venus and 70024 Vulcan. These were to replace four Jubilee 4-6-0s and were put onto station pilot duties whilst acting as standby locomotives for the mainline services which were diesel-hauled at that time. The active period was from October 1962 until February 1963, after which time the four engines returned to 21D Aston.
Late Hugh Ballantyne/Rail Photoprints

70023
VENUS
70023

Having gone to Old Oak Common as a new engine fresh from Crewe in the summer of 1951, 70023 Venus and was one of the Britannias drafted on to the Southern Region for a month in May 1953, after a number of the Merchant Navy class were stopped with axle problems. With 70023 being based at Salisbury during this short period of time. Once returned here to Old Oak Common we see her by the coaling stage around 1956. Before seeing her again after transfer to the LMR heading south from Lancaster with an up parcels train in July 1963.
Photos: Rail Online & Dave Cobbe Collection/Rail Photoprints

Recently outshopped from Crewe Works in the economy green livery 70024 Vulcan finds itself stabled at Bristol's Barrow Road shed on 27 June 1964. Just a few weeks earlier in May 1964, 70025 Western Star runs off shed at Patricroft, although there was a large gap between their introductions into service as 70025 Western Star was completed almost twelve months after 70024 Vulcan; this delay was due to an acute shortage of steel following on from World War Two, however, this delay gave those at Crewe Works an opportunity to apply the modifications found to be necessary during the service period of those earlier twenty-five engines.
Colour Rail & Late Jim Carter/Rail Photoprints

70025

On 20 November 1955, 70026 Polar Star was hauling an excursion train that was derailed at Milton, near Didcot due to excessive speed through a crossover, tragically eleven people were killed and one-hundred-and-fifty-seven even were injured, which was in part attributed to the original style of handrails impairing the driver's forward visibility. Perhaps 70026 Polar Star was seen as a troublesome alien Pacific amongst Swindon's homegrown 4-6-0s whilst on shed at 82C Swindon on 20 September 1959, she appears once again on 17 April 1962 between duties at Willesden.
Colour Rail & Strathwood Library Collection

Opposite: In sparkling condition 70027 Rising Star heads a southbound parcels train running under Class C lamps at Winwick. She had just been transferred from Cardiff Canton to Aston shed in Birmingham after completion of a Heavy General repair at Swindon in September 1961.
Rail Online

70027
70027

Standards were definitely falling by the time of this scene at Crewe in 1964, as not only has 70027 Rising Star fallen on hard times with a lack of any recent cleaning but it seems there are not even enough 6J Holyhead shed plates left to go around. Having been displaced from the Western Region, 70028 Royal Star has no problems with this fitted freight heading through Gerrards Cross on 21 July 1962, now she has just be reallocated to 9A Longsight. ***Photos: Rail Photoprints & Colour Rail***

70028
ROYAL STAR

Seen just a few months before our previous view of 70028 Royal Star, she looks much fitter to wear the name when seen at Manchester Piccadilly on 13 April 1962. ***Colour Rail***

Opposite: A rather mundane duty for 70029 Shooting Star on 10 March 1956, running into Bath Spa with the 05:05 parcels from London to the West of England, whilst on the books at 86C Cardiff Canton. ***Rail Online***

70029

On 13 March 1957, 70030 William Wordsworth was posed for this official photograph at the platform ends of Liverpool Street station during its stint on the Great Eastern routes. However, 70030 began her career working from 6J Holyhead along with 70031, 70032 & 70033, but it was said that the seven-ton coal capacity of the BR1 tender was insufficient to haul the Irish Mail express up to London and return to Holyhead. Likewise, 70031 Byron with a questionable coal capacity was also moved on to 9A Longsight after just eight weeks. Here they were put to work on the Manchester to Euston services including the prestigious Mancunian. The runs to London were found to be no problem and certainly as there were no steep inclines to overcome, and they worked side by side with Royal Scots doing the same turns and therefore were perhaps deemed no better than the 4-6-0s by many of the crews. That basically summed up the effect of the Britannias on the London Midland Region...they were newer locomotives, but only performed to the same levels as many of the 4-6-0 Royal Scot Class engines to which the crews were more familiar to firing and driving. In 1963, 70031 stands alone at Chester back on the North Wales route once again. ***Strathwood Library Collection & Rail Photoprints***

70031
BYRON
70031

As a familiar sight on the West Coast Main Line from 1953 until 1960, 70032 Tennyson would have worked many times between Manchester and Euston. On a very hot day in late July 1957, she waits light engine at the top of Camden Bank. Transfer to 9E Trafford Park shed, also in Manchester in early 1960, meant that 70032 was now to be seen on the former Midland Railway's route to London for a while before being re-allocated to 1A Willesden a year later where we see her moving about the shed limits. Thus in addition to working the Mancunian, it is likely 70032 also saw service on The Thames-Clyde Express and The Palatine named expresses too. During its career 70032 Tennyson, visited Crewe Works fourteen times and is not recorded as entering any other railway works, which would explain why the smoke deflectors were not altered at all, being one of sixteen Britannias that were not changed. ***Photos: Tony Butcher & Rail Photoprints***

70032
TENNYSON
70032

Some of the Britannias were well photographed during their service days and among their number, we must include 70032 Tennyson, seen in this instance on shed at 26F Patricroft during 1961. Then again bursting through Leighton Buzzard with an up express on 23 June 1962. After 1965 when the Britannia class nameplates were removed for safekeeping, 70032 was chosen for a number of railtours and so a set of replica style nameplates were fitted and these were as 'LORD TENNYSON' instead of the original. ***Steve Armitage Archive/Rail Photoprints & Peter Simmonds***

1A30

70033
CHARLES DICKENS
70033

Whereas, 70033 Charles Dickens seems to have been less photographed as it went about its business on British Railways. In 1960 it was photographed between turns at 26F Patricroft, whilst it was allocated to 9E Trafford Park. Likewise 70034 Thomas Hardy was also perhaps a trifle shy to some it seems too in its earlier days. We track 70034 down one day in 1959 on shed at 30A Stratford just as the diesels were beginning to invade in force. ***Both: Rail Online***

On 10 June 1964, 70034 Thomas Hardy was on its home shed of 1A Willesden in fine fettle, ten days later and the locomotive was re-allocated to 5A Crewe North. On another day in 1964, 70035 Rudyard Kipling ponders its next move whilst sitting it out amongst all the grime and soot-laden air at 5B Crewe South.
Photos: Late Hugh Ballantyne/Railphotoprints & Rail Online

8X05

The sight of a Britannia waiting in the sunshine on the servicing road at Liverpool Street station has stirred many a cameraman through the years, one day in 1957 it was the turn of 70036 Boadicea to catch the eye. The mid-1950s was the heyday for the Britannias on the Great Eastern routes from here, hauling express trains such as the Easterling, the Norfolkman, the East Anglian and the Day Continental. Another Britannia familiar to these once great named trains was 70037 Hereward The Wake. It was selected as the engine to represent the class at the International Railway Congress Exhibition held at Willesden, so that over the next three years 70037 was always kept spick and span and used for special trains whenever possible, but from 1957 onwards the locomotive gradually lost its sparkle and became as grubby as the rest of the Britannias, as we see here at Huddersfield in 1961. ***Both: Rail Photoprints***

1F61
70037

70037
RAILWAYS

Opposite: After being repainted into an economy un-lined green livery during its last visit to Crewe Works, 70037 Hereward the Wake languishes within the smoky confines of Patricroft shed, one evening in 1964. Withdrawal came officially on 5 November 1966, but the engine had not turned a wheel since early October 1965, when 70037 suffered wheel-shift. It was then stored at Carlisle Kingmoor until December 1967, finally, the engine was cut up at J. McWilliams of Shettleston during February 1968.
Late Jim Carter/Rail Photoprints

The driver of 70038 Robin Hood puts on a quick turn of speed light engine through Lincoln in 1963. Having started out when new at 30A Stratford, transfer firstly to 32A Norwich came in 1959 and then to 31B March took place the following year, by the time of this view 70038 was on the books at 40B Immingham. It would appear somewhat run down soon after, as with all of the Britannias minus their nameplates and encrusted in filth most of the time. However, by the 2 July 1967, 70038 was specially cleaned and dressed up with painted Robin Hood style nameplates by enthusiasts to work the Stephenson Locomotive Society (Midland Area) Electric-Steam Tour. Whilst an AC Electric was responsible for both outward and return legs between Birmingham New Street and Stockport, it was the well turned out 70038 Robin Hood that was in charge of the run over the Pennines via Standedge to York and back. Unfortunately for the tour participants, it was a poor run for the Britannia as the brakes came on two or three times during the journey, presumably from a loss of vacuum pressure within the train.
Rail Online

70038
ROBIN HOOD
70038

Opposite: A well set up and posed night time shot of 70038 Robin Hood in its cleaned up guise at Patricroft, with the cameraman making use of multiple flashes to highlight the locomotive during his time exposure. *Late Jim Carter/Rail Photoprints*

Being turned on the turntable at Kings Cross on 22 February 1962 was Immingham allocated 70039 Sir Christopher Wren as a regular performer on the services to Grimsby from Kings Cross at this time. *Rail Photoprints*

Two of Crewe North's Britannias side by side in early 1965, with 70042 Lord Roberts on an express and 70021 Morning Star on a parcels train. Both were transferred to Crewe South in June of that year when the North shed was closed on 24 May. The name chosen for 70042 recalls Lord Roberts of Kandahar, a fifty-year career soldier in India, Afghanistan and South Africa who was awarded a Victoria Cross, amongst his many other service honours.
Late Jim Carter/Rail Online

Opposite: On 8 August 1964, 70043 Lord Kitchener was to be found alongside this Black Five at Carnforth, it was always a London Midland Region based Britannia, being variously allocated to; Longsight, Toton, Aston, Willesden, Crewe North and finally Crewe South. For Lord Kitchener withdrawal came early, on 7 August 1965 being stored at Crewe South until 27 October 1965, when the move came to T.W.Ward's of Beighton, in Sheffield for cutting up in November 1965.
Strathwood Library Collection

44775
70043

Certainly the two ugly ducklings among the class in their early years were both 70044 seen here at Nuneaton on 31 December 1955, along with 70043 Lord Kitchener, the pair were both fitted with Air Brake equipment as test beds to compare with the normal Britannias with their vacuum brakes, this continued for some time with no conclusive outcome. Returning to the fold as a normal looking Britannia in the Spring of 1957, 70044 was given the name Earl Haig, we see her on shed simmering in the sunshine at Blackpool South on 2 June 1963. This would also be the last of the class to be built with a BR1 tender.

Photos: Colour Rail & Ian Turnbull/Rail Photoprints

1X93
EARL HAIG
70044

70045

The first engine of the third and final batch of Britannias to be constructed at Crewe was released in June 1954 as 70045. It was the first to be coupled with a larger capacity BR1D tender, capable of holding 9 tons of coal, with 4,725 gallons of water and not requiring a tender step or a flexible cab sheet. The name Lord Rowallan was applied in June 1957 along with the new style of British Railways emblem. By the time this scene was recorded at 12B Carlisle Upperby in 1962 the Chief Scout's appearance was below par. Another Britannia to run without a name for an extended period was 70046, which finally became Anzac in September 1959. Here she arrives at Tamworth Low Level with a Euston to Manchester service, in 1960. ***Both: Rail Photoprints***

70047
70047

Although a large number of names were put forward for the Britannias as a class to choose from, sadly, 70047 would remain nameless throughout its life. She looks well turned out for duty in both of these views from the early 1960s, firstly coming off a train at Chester in June 1964, and secondly shunting some horseboxes at Crewe around 1962.
Photos: Late Jim Carter/Rail Photoprints & Rail Online

THE IRISH MAIL
70048
6
SC

Life began at 6J Holyhead for 70048 in July 1954 as part of a small stud of engines to operate both the Irish Mail day and night boat trains, and this was done successfully until November 1959, when 70048 was among the first Britannias to be allocated to 5A Crewe North. On 17 September 1954, the still new and nameless 70048 is seen ready to depart Holyhead on just such a working to Euston. To commemorate the 50th anniversary of their founding, 70048 was named The Territorial Army 1908-1958 in honour of their heroic efforts as a Volunteer Force. The two-line nameplates were unveiled by the Duke of Norfolk at a ceremony held at Euston station on 22 July 1958. This resulted in these rather large cast-aluminium nameplates being fitted to a then immaculate engine that had left Crewe Works just two weeks previously. All of the other nameplates fitted to the Britannias were cast in brass with their backgrounds variously painted in either red or black during their lives. Withdrawal for 70048 came on Saturday 6 May 1967 from Carlisle Kingmoor, she was then stored at Carlisle Kingmoor until the end of September 1967, before being transferred to J.McWilliams of Shettleston, in Glasgow where cutting up took place in March 1968. This yard swallowed up twelve Britannias as scrap.

Photos: Mike Morant Collection & Rail Online

Built in July 1954 at Crewe and withdrawn in December 1967, 70049 Solway Firth managed sixteen allocations during its all too short thirteen-year service life. We can enjoy her first of all passing Worsley in 1962. Before catching 70049 brewing up a good head of steam before leaving Patricroft shed to take up her next duty in October 1964.
Both: Late Jim Carter/Steve Armitage Archive & Rail Photoprints

70049

Recently ex-works from Crewe in the Autumn of 1963, 70050 Firth of Clyde caught the attention of our cameraman who took the opportunity to climb the coaling tower at 5A Crewe North to get an unrestricted view of this shining lined green Britannia on its then home shed.
Late Jim Carter/Rail Online

Opposite: Our same footplate photographer also climbed the ash plant near the coaler at his home shed of Patricroft to record 70051 Firth of Forth being turned in April 1963. Both 70050 and 70051 went new to 66A Polmadie as their first shed allocation. A terrible reminder of the dangers of being a footplatemen is tied to 70051 Firth of Forth, as a tragic incident occurred on 5 June 1965, when the locomotive was hauling a passenger train and a blowback of the fire occurred near Winsford, severely injuring both train crew. Driver Wallace Oakes managed to safely bring the train to a stand, but both he and fireman Gwilym Roberts were severely injured. The courageous driver Wallace Oakes died a week later. He was awarded the George Cross and the Carnegie Hero Trust bronze medal for his actions posthumously, in recognition of his great bravery in bringing his train to a safe and controlled stop. The circumstances of the blow-back came about because the shroud below the chimney came adrift and dropped onto the blastpipe below thus causing serious back pressure, not unknown, but a rare occurrence nonetheless. In 1981, Class 86 locomotive 86260 was later named Wallace Oakes G.C. in his honour. ***Late Jim Carter/Rail Photoprints***

70051
70051
FIRTH OF FORTH

70052
LCGB
FIRTH OF TAY
1X28
70052

Another Britannia to carry a tragic tale was 70052 Firth of Tay, when on 21 January 1960, she was hauling an express passenger train that was derailed at Settle, Yorkshire due to a defect on the locomotive's motion, five people were killed and nine were injured. On 24 April 1965, 70052 was well prepared at St. Pancras to haul the opening and closing legs of the LCGB's Notts and Lincs Rail Tour to and from Nottingham Midland. For one young lad at least it appears that he has just copped 70053 Moray Firth, perhaps he has just cleared his Britannias? For those on the platform at Crewe on 27 July 1963, the 5A Crewe North allocated 70053 is just drawing in with the southbound Lakes Express.

Photos: Colour Rail & David T. Williams

70054

A Duke of Distinction

Opposite: And so to the last of the Britannias to be constructed at Crewe Works, 70054 Dornoch Firth was completed on 13 September 1954, just 3 months short of the four years since 70000 Britannia was built. Construction costs had risen by almost 21% to £25,331. The initial construction order had been authorised on 24 November 1951, However, there were a number of delays due in the main to shortages of steel. We see her on arrival with an up train at Crewe in the early 1960s to be greeted by an enthusiast's family. ***Rail Online***

The sole BR Standard Class 8 4-6-2 Pacific, 71000 Duke of Gloucester with its design credited to the design team led by messrs Riddles, Bond and Cox only came about as a working prototype through a terrible tragedy as a replacement for the destroyed LMS Princess Royal Class locomotive 46202 Princess Anne, which was involved in the Harrow and Wealdstone rail disaster of 1952. With just over a year to go before it was withdrawn, we see 71000 Duke of Gloucester making a stop at Crewe on 24 June 1961. ***Colour Rail***

Opposite: Sadly not much longer to go for 71000 Duke of Gloucester in the summer of 1962 as she is being prepared for her next journey north by her diligent crew on shed at 1B Camden. ***Late John Day/Rail Photoprints***

Above: Alongside a brand new Class 9F 92156 is almost ready for the paint shop at Crewe Works meanwhile 71000 Duke of Gloucester is back in for overhaul in the Autumn of 1957. No doubt for further investigations as to why she had such a poor reputation for steaming and her hunger for coal consumption.
Strathwood Library Collection

Here she is being proudly exhibited in the goods yard at Marylebone in May 1961, during the exhibition to celebrate the 50th anniversary of the Institute of Locomotive Engineers. Although the Duke of Gloucester was based on the design of the two-cylinder Britannias, but incorporating three-cylinders each worked by sets of modified Caprotti valve gear, these were relatively new to British locomotive engineering and more efficient than the traditional Walschaerts or Stephenson valve gear. ***Strathwood Library Collection***

71000
DUKE OF GLOUCESTER
71000

Based for its entire working life at 5A Crewe North, the locomotive was mostly put to use on hauling boat trains on the undemanding North Wales Coast Line between Crewe and Holyhead, this also kept it close to Crewe Works for attention on its rotary poppet driven Caprotti valve gear. This culminated in 71000 Duke of Gloucester having a short service life of only eight years, being withdrawn from service on 24 November 1962. After withdrawal, she was initially selected for the National Collection, though it was later decided that only the cylinder arrangement was of interest. One of the outside cylinders was removed for display at the Science Museum; the other was removed to restore balance in readiness for scrapping. Meanwhile the locomotive had lain firstly at Crewe North and then within the works at Crewe until November 1967 when the locomotive was purchased by Dai Woodham at Barry. In 1974, what was left of the locomotive, having lost its tender, valve gear and just about everything that was non-ferrous was purchased by the Duke of Gloucester Steam Locomotive Trust. After a massive amount of work and fundraising through thirteen years, she was at last brought back to steam as a triumph in preservation. ***Late John Day/Rail Photoprints***

Gathering of the Clans

One of the lessons learnt through the 1948 Locomotive Exchanges, when the Bulleid West Country 34004 Yeovil was tested away from the Southern Region, was its massive route availability for a powerful Pacific. There were advantages of such a locomotive for use on some of the heavily restricted main lines in Scotland, such as the Dumfries to Stranraer line, or the steeply graded ex-Highland Railway line to Inverness. The exchanges showed that a Light Pacific had the potential to revolutionise the timetables over these difficult trunk routes. As the general policy of the Railway Executive was to eliminate as far as possible the perceived complication of multi-cylinder locomotives, an equivalent two-cylinder Pacific was to be produced by mounting a smaller and lighter boiler on the standard 7MT Britannia chassis, thus the design for what became the Clans was born. On 31 July 1959, the first of the class, 72000 Clan Buchanan takes on water during a stop at Carlisle. *Colour Rail*

72000
CLAN BUCHANAN
72000

Opposite: Under the initial scheme for the creation of a series of British Railways standard locomotives, the larger passenger and mixed traffic types were intended to be of the 4-6-2 Pacific wheel arrangement. The main advantage of which was that they could then all be fitted with a wide firebox capable of burning a variety of coal grades and qualities. These Pacifics were originally intended to be produced in four power groups: Classes 8, 7, 6, and 5, according to the system of power ratings inherited from the LMS, with the last three ratings to be regarded as mixed traffic. The whole standardisation programme began with the construction of the 7MT Britannias in 1951. Although the Standard Class 5MT Pacific proposal was dropped in favour of a 4-6-0, the first of what became the Clans as a Class 6MT began with 72000 Clan Buchanan going to take up service at 66A Polmadie in December 1951, here she is on shed there a few years later. ***Rail Photoprints***

The second of the class 72001 Clan Cameron went into traffic again at Polmadie the same month at the close of 1951. One of their regular turns was between Glasgow and Manchester, in the early 1960s we see 72001 drifting past Patricroft's North Sidings on the 16:30 Manchester to Glasgow. Designed at the drawing offices of Derby Works, the Clans were all constructed at Crewe Works between 1951 and 1952. Although the initial order was for twenty-five locomotives, such was the immediacy of demand regarding a smaller version of the Britannia Pacifics that a batch of ten was rushed through construction before any teething problems had been ironed out at the British Railways testing station at Rugby. However, due to acute steel shortages in Britain which also affected the building of the Britannias, the order for the next fifteen Clans was continually postponed, until it was finally cancelled on the publication of the 1955 Modernisation Plan for the re-equipment of British Railways.
Late Jim Carter/Rail Online

72002
CLAN CAMPBELL
72002

A splendid shot of the third of the Clans to be built, 72002 Clan Campbell on her first home shed at 66A Polmadie, the locomotive is looking to be in immaculate condition and almost certainly a view secured not long after she entered service in January 1952. The additional fifteen of the class proposed in the 1952 New Construction Programme, ten for the Scottish Region and five for the Southern Region, did not materialise, however, and the class remained limited, therefore, to just ten with five being allocated from being newly built to Polmadie and five to Carlisle Kingmoor. This distribution of these ten Clans had not been the intention when the original plans were laid for the class, it was intended that they would work the Highland mainline between Perth and Inverness. During their short working lives, the Clans would also be based at both of Edinburgh's main sheds, Haymarket and St. Margarets briefly. Our second view of 72002 Clan Campbell dates from 1961, its penultimate year in traffic whilst on shed at Carlisle Kingmoor.
Photos: Rail Online & Strathwood Library Collection

COMPLETE
HOUSE FURNISHERS
A. GARDNER &
36
72003

Opposite: On 8 August 1953, 72003 Clan Fraser is ready for departure from Glasgow Central towards the English border. Regular duties for spotters to see the Clans at work included; Glasgow to Crewe, Manchester and Liverpool services, Edinburgh to Leeds services, Carlisle to Bradford services, and finally the Stranraer Boat Train workings. ***Colour Rail***

The enginemen at 66A Polmadie did well with their Clans often taking fourteen unaided over Beattock, whilst locomotive crews elsewhere who were less familiar with such a small class complained about their steaming characteristics. This is 72004 Clan MacDonald, at home on Polmadie in November 1957. ***Rail Photoprints***

On a sunny day during 1956, 72005 Clan MacGregor takes a breather between turns on shed at Carstairs. The first five of the class 72000-4 would all be withdrawn from the Scottish Region together in December 1962, leaving 72005-9 to hang on for just a few more years. ***Rail Photoprints***

Opposite: On 30 June 1963, 72006 Clan Mackenzie is about to leave Carlisle Citadel with the 13:05 (Sunday only) Manchester to Glasgow service while alongside Coronation Pacific 46249 City of Sheffield waits to relieve the northbound Royal Scot. ***Late Hugh Ballantyne/Rail Photoprints***

46249
72006

Perhaps with fears that the remaining five Clans would also soon be withdrawn, 72006 Clan MacKenzie was the requested motive power to run the Home Counties Railway Society's special from Paddington to Swindon Works and return on 8 December 1963, here she is looking scruffy at Old Oak Common beforehand, she was only marginally cleaner when actually working the special. ***Colour Rail***

Opposite: Standing alongside Chester No.6 Signal Box in the mid-sixties, having arrived on an early morning local passenger from Manchester, Driver Bill Jones & Fireman Fred Carter await the right away from Chester No.6 signal box to run tender first to Mold Junction where they can take their breakfast. They will return with 72006 Clan MacKenzie on a Mold Junction to Patricroft through goods train. ***Late Jim Carter/Rail Online***

72006

5
72007
CLAN MACKINTOSH
72007

Opposite: Two views of 72007 Clan Mackintosh, firstly soon after entering service in the early 1950s, stabled in the sunshine outside the sheds at Carlisle Kingmoor when it was part of the Scottish Region and coded as 68A. Maintenance was initially undertaken at Crewe Works, but responsibility was transferred to Cowlairs Works in the spring of 1958. With more varied work being allocated to them as their reliability improved and more crews were familiar with working them, including working portions of the Thames-Clyde Express and the Queen of Scots Pullman. They also deputised for the many failed diesel locomotives that plagued the railways at the time and were extensively used on freight workings. Once dieselisation started in earnest in the early 1960s, the Clans were downgraded to secondary work, therefore it is perhaps no surprise that the first five were withdrawn so quickly. *Rail Online*

Most Scottish and Midland Region crews that used them regularly took to the class and found that if used properly, running times were kept with ease. These crews rated them the most sure-footed of any of the Pacifics available on the Midland Region, although other crews who tested them claimed that the Clans were prone to slipping, however, this was the case with most Pacific designs. Despite the various successes of the Clans, the class was generally regarded as a failure, even with overall performance being just short of Riddles' aims. However, the premise of all British Railways Standard designs was for a hard-working, easily maintained, economical, highly available, and all-purpose locomotive. In these respects, the Clans such as 72007 Clan Mackintosh seen here at Carlisle were highly successful. *Colour Rail*

72008

Opposite: Carlisle Kingmoor's 72008 Clan Macleod awaits departure from Glasgow Buchanan Street, whilst a humble Caley 0-4-4T 55222 on station pilot duties brews up in the adjacent platform, sometime in 1956. Both 72007 & 72008 would remain allocated to Kingmoor throughout their lives. ***Rail Photoprints***

The last of the Clans to be built by British Railways would be 72009 Clan Stewart seen here out in the yard at Glasgow Balornock (St. Rollox) in 1957, note the brazier hanging down ready to be lit in cold weather to help prevent the turntable's bearing freezing up. ***Rail Photoprints***

ABINGTON
CHANGE HERE FOR

Up Close

In August 1958, 72009 Clan Stewart was tested on the Eastern Region, being based at 30A Stratford until October for trials on the former Great Eastern routes. Although the Eastern Region had a preference for the Britannias already allocated there, this meant that this trial would be short-lived with the Clan rated on a par with a good Class B1. Even so 72009 Clan Stewart was utilised on services from Liverpool Street to Norwich, Clacton, and Harwich. This lowly duty back on Scottish Region metals on 8 October 1963, will hardly test her on the 09:10 Carlisle to Glasgow Central service calling at Abington.
Late Hugh Ballantyne-Rail Photoprints

As with many classes of locomotive through the years, further experience and development would bring changes to the Standard Pacifics. The most notable perhaps would be around the design of the smoke deflectors as fitted to the Britannias. Here 70033 Charles Dickens retains the original style when recorded on shed at Patricroft in the mid-sixties, it's sadly now dressed in the economy green livery without any lining out.
Late Jim Carter/Rail Online

Whilst examining the front ends of the Britannias, we should also mention some of the many differences in the positioning of lamp irons through their careers as they were adapted to new shed allocations requirements. Here an almost new 70006 Robert Burns is seen at Liverpool Street in the summer of 1951. Compare with 70049 Solway Firth at Patricroft in November 1963, we can see also differences in the style of vacuum pipe, a protection plate for the ATC/AWS behind the coupling, and the modified front step below the smoke box to allow footplate men easier access to the top lamp bracket.
Photos: Rail Photoprints & Rail Online

70049
SOLWAY FIRTH

The Britannias allocated to the Western Region and overhauled at Swindon had their smoke deflector modifications with six cut-outs in each deflector sheet. The majority of these handholds were brass-lined, which added to the overall look of the engines, being usually kept in very clean condition by staff at Cardiff Canton. The nine locomotives so treated were: 70015, 70016, 70018, 70019, 70022, 70023, 70025, 70026 & 70027. In this view of 70016 Ariel ex-works at Swindon in June 1956, the new style of British Railways emblem has also just been applied, note also the mix of fluted and solid coupling rods. Another of the Western Region modified Britannias, 70022 Tornado is seen at Cardiff Canton in April 1960. ***Photos: Rail Photoprints & Colour Rail***

Although sixteen Britannias retained their original smoke deflectors throughout their lives, essentially those that were maintained at Crewe Works, Nos. 70004, 70014, 70021, 70031, 70032, 70033, 70042, 70043, 70045, 70046, 70047, 70048, 70049, 70050, 70051 & 70052. Twenty-five engines received this modification as modelled by 70010 Owen Glendower and 70012 John of Gaunt. The offending handrails were also removed, being replaced by two handholds with backing cups, the first to be modified was 70038 Robin Hood which entered Doncaster Works in November 1957, and emerged in December suitably modified. This started off a programme whereby all the Great Eastern section Britannias were altered within two years. The last of the class to be treated with modified deflectors was

70044 Earl Haig in July 1960, also at Doncaster, however, it is worth mentioning that this example was fitted with Westinghouse Brake Equipment from almost new and was not fitted with any smoke deflectors until March 1957. Interestingly Swindon Works also fitted this type of hand holds but without the backing cups, to Nos. 70017, 70020, 70024, 70028 & 70029, these being modified between late 1957 and early 1959. Notably, although 70021 Morning Star was on the Western Region for seven years, she was not changed in any way, and 70042 Lord Robert was allocated to the former Great Eastern section for almost five years, also missed out being altered too. ***Both: Strathwood Library Collection***

Two views of 70046 Anzac taken at Patricroft whilst it was allocated to 6J Holyhead between December 1962 and February 1965 from the camera of the late Jim Carter at his home shed. They serve to show us the head on view of those offending smoke deflectors and the missing protective plate behind the coupling shielding the ATC/AWS pick up gear. The view opposite shows the positioning of the AWS battery boxes on the running plate. We should also note that the coupling rods on 70046 Anzac are of the stronger solid milled variety. These are just a few of the variations and modifications that were to be seen during the Britannias seventeen-year working lives. ***Both: Late Jim Carter/Rail Online***

70046

Above: The front smoke box step was also altered on 71000 Duke of Gloucester to allow easier access for footplate crews to the top lamp bracket for both affixing lamps and as seen here at Euston on 4 May 1957 named train headboards, such as today's Mid-Day Scot.
Strathwood Library Collection

This view inside Crewe North shed during 1962 shows 71000 Duke of Gloucester with the modified step, but sadly now out of traffic and in storage, the front coupling and the vacuum pipe are missing, however it does reveal the AWS protection plate.
Late Colin Whitfield/Rail Photoprints

Opposite: This view of 72007 Clan Mackintosh at Perth on 14 August 1961, shows the rubberised sheeting provided to help reduce the complaints of cold draughts on the footplates of both Britannias and Clans which caused coal-dust storms for the locomotive crews on the BR1 tenders.
Rail Online

72007
BRITISH

70013

The last years of the surviving Britannias and the Clans saw them in traffic more often than not in a very rundown state. Sadly without the dignity of its nameplates 70013, Oliver Cromwell stands on the turntable at Patricroft, in July 1966 whilst at least being clean and retaining its lining it looks more appealing than 70025 Western Star being explored unofficially whilst on shed at Carnforth on 30 April 1966.
Photos: Late Jim Carter/Rail Photoprints & Strathwood Library Collection

Above & Opposite: For 70047 it was never to have the distinction of being named during its working life, we see it being moved around 5A Crewe North shed in the early 1960s complete with its lined out BR1D tender as originally fitted to Nos. 70045-54. Although by 26 March 1967, 70014 has lost its Iron Duke nameplates in favour of painted replacements, and has gained a BR1D tender having lost its original BR1 tender to 70013. ***Photos: Rail Online & Rail Photoprints***

70014

When originally built 71000 Duke of Gloucester was given a BR1E tender which was basically the same as the BR1D tenders as fitted to the last batch of Britannias, except the coal capacity was increased by 1 ton up to 10 tons, with the same water capacity of 4,725 gallons it was also fitted with the same style of coal pusher. However, it was decided in service that the coal capacity should be increased further, therefore another unique tender designated BR1J was produced for the locomotive in November 1957. This new tender held nominally the same amount of coal but further to the rear as there may have been clearance issues, thus reducing the water capacity to 4,325 gallons, the flares of this second tender extended further to the rear, as seen here at Crewe on 18 August 1962. ***Colour Rail***